NOW
PANIC

AND

FREAK
OUT

NOW
PANIC

AND

FREAK
OUT

NOW
PANIC

AND

FREAK
OUT

NO
PANI

AND

FREA
UT

NOW
PANIC

AND

FREAK
OUT

NOW
PANIC

AND

FREAK
OUT

NOW
PANIC

AND

FREAK
OUT

NO
PAN

AND

FREA
OUT

NOW
PANIC

AND

FREAK
UT

NOW
PANIC

AND

FREAK
OUT

NOW
PANIC

AND

FREAK
OUT

NO
PANI

AND

FREAK
OUT

NOW
PANIC

AND

FREAK
OUT

NOW
PANIC

AND

FREAK
OUT

NOW
PANIC

AND

FREAK
OUT

N
PA

AN

FREA
OUT

D0445396

NOW PANIC AND FREAK OUT NOW PANIC AND FREAK OUT NOW PANIC AND FREAK OUT NOW PANIC AND FREAK OUT

NOW PANIC AND FREAK OUT NOW PANIC AND FREAK OUT NOW PANIC AND FREAK OUT NOW PANIC AND FREAK OUT

NOW PANIC AND FREAK OUT NOW PANIC AND FREAK OUT NOW PANIC AND FREAK OUT NOW PANIC AND FREAK OUT

NOW PANIC AND FREAK OUT NOW PANIC AND FREAK OUT NOW PANIC AND FREAK OUT NOW PANIC AND FREAK OUT

NOW
PANIC
AND
FREAK
OUT

summersdale

NOW PANIC AND FREAK OUT

Summersdale Publishers Ltd
46 West Street
Chichester
West Sussex
PO19 1RP
UK

www.summersdale.com

Printed and bound in the Czech Republic

ISBN: 978-1-84953-103-0

Substantial discounts on bulk quantities of Summersdale books are available to corporations, professional associations and other organisations. For details contact Summersdale Publishers by telephone: +44 (0) 1243 771107, fax: +44 (0) 1243 786300 or email: nicky@summersdale.com.

NOW
PANIC
AND
FREAK
OUT

When in danger or in doubt, run in circles, scream and shout.

Robert A. Heinlein

Anyone who isn't confused
really doesn't understand
the situation.

Edward R. Murrow

We experience moments
absolutely free from worry.
These brief respites are
called panic.

Cullen Hightower

We live in a
rainbow of chaos.

Paul Cézanne

Don't let ageing get
you down. It's too
hard to get back up.

John Wagner

Hi-tech tomatoes. Super squash. Are we supposed to eat this stuff? Or is it going to eat us?

Annita Manning

Every faculty… I possess
can be used as an
instrument with which to
worry myself.

Mark Rutherford

There's a fine line between genius and insanity. I have erased this line.

Oscar Levant

Try not to worry…
take each day just one
anxiety attack at
a time.

Tom Wilson

A question that sometimes drives me hazy: am I or are the others crazy?

Albert Einstein

I don't want to retire.
I'm not that good at
crossword puzzles.

Norman Mailer

Love looks forward, hate looks back, anxiety has eyes all over its head.

Mignon McLaughlin

I think that was a
moment of cool
panic there.

Ron Atkinson

A word to the wise ain't
necessary – it's the stupid
ones that need the advice.

Bill Cosby

We are, perhaps, uniquely among the earth's creatures, the worrying animal.

Lewis Thomas

I accept chaos. I'm not
sure whether it
accepts me.

Bob Dylan

What sane person
could live in this world
and not be crazy?

Ursula K. LeGuin

It's nice to see that look of
alarm on the faces of
the others.

Graham Chapman

The reason why worry kills
more people than work is
that more people worry
than work.

Robert Frost

Exercise daily. Eat
wisely. Die anyway.

Anonymous

Don't worry that children
never listen to you; worry
that they are always
watching you.

Robert Fulghum

Life is not a spectacle
or a feast; it is a
predicament.

George Santayana

Laugh at yourself first,
before anyone
else can.

Elsa Maxwell

Dread of disaster makes
everybody act in the very
way that increases
the disaster.

Bertrand Russell

You have to go on and
be crazy. Craziness
is like heaven.

Jimi Hendrix

Every day I run scared.
That's the only way I can
stay ahead.

John H. Johnson

Better mad with the rest of the world than wise alone.

Baltasar Gracián

Leadership has been
defined as the ability to hide
your panic from others.

Anonymous

To live is so startling
it leaves little time for
anything else.

Emily Dickinson

The only thing to do with
good advice is to pass it on.
It is never of any use
to oneself.

Oscar Wilde

Speak when you're angry,
and you'll make the best
speech you'll ever regret.

Lawrence J. Peter

When you become
senile, you won't
know it.

Bill Cosby

When one has too great a
dread of what is impending,
one feels some relief when
the trouble has come.

Joseph Joubert

A zebra does not
change its spots.

Al Gore

Insanity: doing the same thing over and over again and expecting different results.

Albert Einstein

Experience is a
terrible teacher who
sends horrific bills.

Anonymous

They couldn't hit an elephant at this dist–

**The last words of
General John Sedgwick**

I owe my success to having listened respectfully to the very best advice, and then going away and doing the exact opposite.

G. K. Chesterton

Do not take life too
seriously. You will
never get out of
it alive.

Elbert Hubbard

If crime went down 100 per cent, it would still be 50 times higher than it should be.

John Bowman

Only one man ever understood me, and he didn't understand me.

G. W. Hegel

I used to believe that
anything was better than
nothing. Now I know that
sometimes nothing is better.

Glenda Jackson

The only thing that remains unsolved is the resolution of the problem.

Thomas Wells

Life is rather like a tin of sardines – we're all of us looking for the key.

Alan Bennett

If one synchronised swimmer drowns, do the rest have to drown too?

Steven Wright

Never worry about
your heart till it stops
beating.

E. B. White

The past is the only dead thing that smells sweet.

Cyril Connolly

Moderation is a fatal thing.
Nothing succeeds
like excess.

Oscar Wilde

Make somebody happy today. Mind your own business.

Ann Landers

Life – a spiritual pickle
preserving the body
from decay.

Ambrose Bierce

Technological progress has merely provided us with more efficient means for going backwards.

Aldous Huxley

We live in an age
when pizza gets to
your home before
the police.

Jeff Marder

In this world, nothing is
certain but death and taxes.

Benjamin Franklin

The perfect normal
person is rare in
our civilisation.

Karen Horney

It's all right letting yourself go as long as you can let yourself back.

Mick Jagger

Insanity is hereditary;
you get it from your
children.

Sam Levenson

Life is a zoo in a jungle.

Peter De Vries

I have a simple philosophy:
Fill what's empty. Empty
what's full. Scratch where
it itches.

Alice Roosevelt Longworth

The future we're leaving
our children is less an
ecological legacy, more a
pre-emptive strike.

Rob Newman

If things go wrong,
don't go with them.

Roger Babson

Life is a rollercoaster. Try to eat a light lunch.

David A. Schmaltz

Say what you will about the Ten Commandments, you must always come back to the pleasant fact that there are only ten of them.

H. L. Mencken

The difference between life and the movies is that a script has to make sense, and life doesn't.

Joseph L. Mankiewicz

Time you enjoy wasting, was not wasted.

John Lennon

Don't look where you fall, but where you slipped.

African proverb

Clothes make the man.
Naked people have little or
no influence on society.

Mark Twain

Most cars on the roads have only one occupant, usually the driver.

Carol Malia

I am free of all prejudices. I hate everyone equally.

W. C. Fields

I've got to follow them;
I am their leader.

Alexandre Ledru-Rollin

Experience is the name
everyone gives to
their mistakes.

Oscar Wilde

God is good, but
never dance in a
small boat.

Irish proverb

We must believe in free will
– we have no choice.

Isaac Bashevis Singer

If history repeats itself, and the unexpected always happens, how incapable must Man be of learning from experience.

George Bernard Shaw

I've read about foreign policy and studied. I now know the number of continents.

George Wallace

Advice is what we ask for
when we already know the
answer but wish we didn't.

Erica Jong

Never saw off the
branch you are on,
unless you are being
hanged from it.

Stanislaw J. Lec

You want to run out in front,
prepare to be tripped
from behind.

S. A. Sachs

In the long run
we are all dead.

John Maynard Keynes

Don't ever take a
fence down until you
know why it was
put up.

Robert Frost

I don't think you ever know in yourself whether you have gone mad.

Chris Lowe

Facts are stupid things.

Ronald Reagan

It only seems as if you are
doing something when
you're worrying.

Lucy Maud Montgomery

Life is the farce which everyone has to perform.

Arthur Rimbaud

The first half of our lives is
ruined by our parents and
the second half by
our children.

Clarence Darrow

Multimedia? As far as I'm concerned, it's reading with the radio on!

Rory Bremner

Real difficulties can be overcome, it is only the imaginary ones that are unconquerable.

Theodore N. Vail

I hope life isn't a big
joke, because I
don't get it.

Jack Handey

If you haven't set off yet, the best thing to do is turn back and go home.

Anne Nightingale

Science in the modern world
has many uses; its chief
use, however, is to provide
long words to cover the
errors of the rich.

G. K. Chesterton

Caution: cape does not enable user to fly.

Warning label on a Batman costume

I am an old man and
have known a great many
troubles, but most of them
never happened.

Mark Twain

Any idiot can face a crisis – it's day to day living that wears you out.

Anton Chekhov

Not a shred of evidence
exists in favour of the idea
that life is serious.

Brendan Gill

Ignorance more
frequently begets
confidence than does
knowledge.

Charles Darwin

I've been absolutely terrified
every moment of my life.

Georgia O'Keeffe

Life is very interesting
if you make mistakes.

Georges Carpentier

Everything has been
figured out, except
how to live.

Jean-Paul Sartre

There was never yet an uninteresting life. Such a thing is an impossibility. Inside of the dullest exterior there is a drama, a comedy and a tragedy.

Mark Twain

China is a big
country, inhabited by
many Chinese.

Charles de Gaulle

If the world should blow itself up, the last audible voice would be that of an expert saying it can't be done.

Peter Ustinov

And in the end, it's not the years in your life that count. It's the life in your years.

Abraham Lincoln

Real life seems
to have no plots.

Ivy Compton-Burnett

If Abraham Lincoln
were alive now, he'd
roll over in his grave.

Gerald Ford

I have opinions of my own,
strong opinions, but I don't
always agree with them.

George W. Bush

Life is one fool thing after
another whereas love is two
fool things after each other.

Oscar Wilde

Life is divided into
the horrible and the
miserable.

Woody Allen

For peace of mind, resign as
general manager of
the universe.

Larry Eisenberg

I'm an atheist,
thank God.

Luis Buñuel

Suicide is a real threat
to health in modern
society.

Virginia Bottomley

I have left orders to be awakened at any time in case of national emergency – even if I'm in a Cabinet meeting.

Ronald Reagan

We've got to pause and ask
ourselves: how much clean
air do we need?

Lee Iacocca

The art of living is more like wrestling than dancing.

Marcus Aurelius

The time to begin most
things is ten years ago.

Mignon McLaughlin

The purpose of life is
to fight maturity.

Dick Werthimer

The tide is very much
in our court now.

Kevin Keegan

Experience is a comb that
life gives you after you
lose your hair.

Judith Stern

I used to eat a lot of natural foods until I learned that most people die of natural causes.

Anonymous

All life is an experiment.

Ralph Waldo Emerson

Politics gives guys so much power that they tend to behave badly around women. And I hope I never get into that.

Bill Clinton

In the Soviet army it takes more courage to retreat than advance.

Joseph Stalin

Osama Bin Laden is
either alive and well,
or alive and not well,
or not alive.

Donald Rumsfeld

Life can only be understood
backwards; but it must
be lived forwards.

Søren Kierkegaard

I love deadlines. I like the
whooshing sound they make
as they fly by.

Douglas Adams

When things are perfect, that's when you need to worry most.

Drew Barrymore

If we weren't all crazy,
we'd just go insane.

Jimmy Buffett

When one subtracts from
life infancy (which is
vegetation), sleep, eating
and swilling, buttoning
and unbuttoning – how
much remains of downright
existence? The summer
of a dormouse.

Lord Byron

Hard work never killed
anybody, but why
take a chance?

Edgar Bergen

Never put off until tomorrow
what you can do the day
after tomorrow.

Mark Twain

Death is one of the
few things that can
be done just as easily
lying down.

Woody Allen

It may be that your sole
purpose in life is simply to
serve as a warning
to others.

John Kirinrich

Just because nobody
complains doesn't mean all
parachutes are perfect.

Benny Hill

The trouble with the
rat race is that even if
you win you're still
a rat.

Lily Tomlin

Life is a horizontal fall.

Jean Cocteau

Constantly choosing the lesser of two evils is still choosing evil.

Jerry Garcia

We are not retreating – we are advancing in another direction.

Douglas MacArthur

I think they've
misunderestimated
me.

George W. Bush

To lose one parent...
may be regarded as a
misfortune; to lose both
looks like carelessness.

Oscar Wilde

I don't suffer from insanity. I enjoy every minute of it.

Anonymous

You know, solving other people's problems is easy. The only person I can't seem to figure out is myself.

Thomas James Higgins

You're only given
a little spark of
madness. You mustn't
lose it.

Robin Williams

Living in continual chaos is exhausting, frightening. The catch is that it's also very addictive.

Lorna Luft

In a mad world,
only the mad
are sane.

Akira Kurosawa

My experience is that as soon as people are old enough to know better, they don't know anything at all.

Oscar Wilde

The Tory party only
panics in a crisis.

Iain MacLeod

Correct me if I'm wrong, but hasn't the fine line between sanity and madness gotten finer?

George Price

Two things are infinite:
the universe and human
stupidity; and I'm not sure
about the universe.

Albert Einstein

Forget the past – the
future will give you
plenty to worry about.

George Allen

Be careful about reading
health books. You may die
of a misprint.

Mark Twain

The email of the
species is more
deadly than the mail.

Stephen Fry

The people who know how to run the country are busy driving taxicabs and cutting hair.

George Burns

The man who smiles
when things go
wrong has thought of
someone to blame
it on.

Robert Bloch

Time is a great teacher, but
unfortunately it kills
all of its pupils.

Louis Hector Berlioz

Most accidents occur within
five minutes of the home.
Move house.

Milton Berle

Life isn't fair. It's just fairer than death, that's all.

William Goldman

KEEP
CALM

AND

DRINK
UP

KEEP CALM AND DRINK UP

£4.99

ISBN: 978 1 84953 102 3

'*In victory, you deserve champagne; in defeat, you need it.*'

Napoleon Bonaparte

BAD ADVICE FOR GOOD PEOPLE.

Keep Calm and Carry On, a World War Two government poster, struck a chord in recent difficult times when a stiff upper lip and optimistic energy were needed again. But in the long run it's a stiff drink and flowing spirits that keep us all going.

Here's a book packed with proverbs and quotations showing the wisdom to be found at the bottom of the glass.

Have you enjoyed this book? If so, why not write a review on your favourite website?

Thanks very much for buying this Summersdale book.

www.summersdale.com

NOW PANIC AND FREAK OUT NOW PANIC AND FREAK OUT NOW PANIC AND FREAK OUT NOW PANIC AND FREAK OUT

NOW PANIC AND FREAK OUT NOW PANIC AND FREAK OUT NOW PANIC AND FREAK OUT NOW PANIC AND FREAK OUT

NOW PANIC AND FREAK OUT NOW PANIC AND FREAK OUT NOW PANIC AND FREAK OUT NOW PANIC AND FREAK OUT

NOW PANIC AND FREAK OUT NOW PANIC AND FREAK OUT NOW PANIC AND FREAK OUT NOW PANIC AND FREAK OUT

NOW PANIC AND FREAK OUT

NOW PANIC AND FREAK OUT

NOW PANIC AND FREAK OUT

NOW PANIC AND FREAK OUT

NOW PANIC AND FREAK OUT

NOW PANIC AND FREAK OUT

NOW PANIC AND FREAK OUT

NOW PANIC AND FREAK OUT

NOW PANIC AND FREAK OUT

NOW PANIC AND FREAK OUT

NOW PANIC AND FREAK OUT

NOW PANIC AND FREAK OUT

NOW PANIC AND FREAK OUT

NOW PANIC AND FREAK OUT

NOW PANIC AND FREAK OUT

NOW PANIC AND FREAK OUT